Uniting Generations
A FRIENDS & FAMILY DEVOTIONAL

Harris House
Publishing

Torch Runner Publications
An Imprint of Harris House Publishing

Uniting Generations: A Friends & Family Devotional
Copyright ©2020 by Harris House Publishing
Edited and Compiled by Sherri West Coats

Published by Torch Runner Publications
An Imprint of Harris House Publishing
harrishousepublishing.com
Colleyville, Texas, USA

Scripture quotations marked NKJV are taken from the New King James Version®. Copyright © 1982 by Thomas Nelson. Used by permission. All rights reserved.
Scripture quotations marked NIV are taken from the Holy Bible, New International Version®, NIV®. Copyright © 1973, 1978, 1984, 2011 by Biblica, Inc.™ Used by permission of Zondervan. All rights reserved worldwide. www.zondervan.com The "NIV" and "New International Version" are trademarks registered in the United States Patent and Trademark Office by Biblica, Inc.™
Scripture quotations marked NLT are taken from the Holy Bible, New Living Translation, copyright ©1996, 2004, 2015 by Tyndale House Foundation. Used by permission of Tyndale House Publishers, a Division of Tyndale House Ministries, Carol Stream, Illinois 60188. All rights reserved.
Scripture quotations marked TPT are from The Passion Translation®. Copyright © 2017, 2018 by Passion & Fire Ministries, Inc. Used by permission. All rights reserved. ThePassionTranslation.com.
Scripture quotations marked ESV are from the ESV® Bible (The Holy Bible, English Standard Version®), copyright © 2001 by Crossway, a publishing ministry of Good News Publishers. Used by permission. All rights reserved.
Scripture quotations marked NASB are taken from the New American Standard Bible® (NASB), Copyright © 1960, 1962, 1963, 1968, 1971, 1972, 1973, 1975, 1977, 1995 by The Lockman Foundation. Used by permission. www.Lockman.org
Scripture quotations marked HCSB are taken from the Holman Christian Standard Bible®, Used by Permission HCSB ©1999,2000,2002,2003,2009 Holman Bible Publishers. Holman Christian Standard Bible®, Holman CSB®, and HCSB® are federally registered trademarks of Holman Bible Publishers.
Scripture quotations marked CEV are from the Contemporary English Version Copyright © 1991, 1992, 1995 by American Bible Society. Used by Permission.
Scripture quotations marked MSG are taken from THE MESSAGE, copyright © 1993, 2002, 2018 by Eugene H. Peterson. Used by permission of NavPress. All rights reserved. Represented by Tyndale House Publishers, a Division of Tyndale House Ministries.
Scripture quotations marked ASV are taken from the American Standard Version, public domain. Scripture quotations marked KJV are taken from the King James Version, public domain.

All devotions printed by permission of individual contributors.
ISBN: 978-1-946369-00-0
Subject heading: DEVOTIONAL LITERATURE/FAMILY/CHRISTIAN LIFE

All rights reserved. No portion of this book may be produced, stored in a retrieval system or transmitted in any form or by any means—electronic, mechanical, photocopy, recording, or any other—except by the individual authors of each devotional, without the prior permission of the publisher.
Printed in the United States of America.

EDITH & FORREST HARRIS
GROUSE MOUNTAIN CHAIR LIFT
VANCOUVER, CANADA

Dedication

This work is dedicated to every aunt, uncle, parent, grandparent, and great-grandparent who was faithful to the Gospel of Jesus Christ, who intentionally passed their faith to the next generation, and who is now spending eternity in heaven.

We are eternally grateful to the many Harris family members who have gone on before us, who actively and purposely lived out their faith in a way that led us to Jesus. Your fingerprints of love and grace have made a lasting imprint on our lives. Your example has been an inspiration and a guiding light. Because of you, we too, will tell the next generation of His mighty acts. Psalms 145:4

Forrest & Edith Harris with their seven children, circa 1960

Ada Connection is a family and friends reunion, which takes place once every five years in Ada, Oklahoma. It represents a group of people who have served God and lived life together for generations. *Uniting Generations* is a devotional book resulting from Ada Connection 2020. Its contributors are descendants of Forrest and Edith Harris and their seven children: Vern Harris, Glenn Harris, Ralph Harris, Genevieve Harris Debord Blenkhorn, Nellie May Harris Weidenhamer, Patricia Harris Kauffman, Darleene Harris Hemmerling, and individuals who are connected to the Harris family through marriage or friendship. This work is a testament to God's faithfulness throughout the generations.

The Harris Family's Spiritual Journey

As Written by Vern Harris, circa January 1998

The start of this story was over 70 years ago, and most of the details are clear in my mind; what bothers me is that I can't remember where I laid my hammer 15 minutes ago. Of necessity, this story is about a family without which there would be no story. The real story I want to emphasize is about a group of people that by their dedication and commitment to the Lord caused the direction of this family to change course and to become what it is today: a beautiful family. I will therefore not name names of the family except for the original seven and the two that came later and some others that have some connection to the story.

Our story begins on a beautiful summer Sunday morning in 1924. Daddy is driving us down the streets of Santa Monica, California, to Sunday School. We are purring along in our 1917 Buick touring car. The 4" x 34" high pressure tires don't give the softest ride in the world, and the heavy wood-spoke wheels have become a little dried out so they are a little loose on the hubs and make a clickety-clack sound when we turn a corner. Daddy is smoking his pipe filled with Prince Albert tobacco. It has to be Prince Albert; that's all he ever smokes. This is not the short-stemmed fashionable pipes of the day, but a large curved stemmed pipe that goes down to a large bowl. It looks like a small saxophone. The breeze caused by the open car is causing a small stream of embers from the burning tobacco to blow from the pipe bowl from time to time. Someone passing by in the other direction might think we have a charcoal burner instead of a gasoline-powered car. Daddy goes serenely down the street taking care of his driving, paying no attention to the flying embers, although in the past he had set himself on fire several times. (After he gave his heart to the Lord Jesus, he threw the pipe away.) We arrive at this large beautiful church, one of the largest in the city. Daddy lets us off on the sidewalk in front of the church and is on his way. Although Momma and Daddy were both raised in church-going families, I can never remember ever seeing them in any kind of a church from as far back as I can remember, and I am the oldest of these five children....

After a short stint at farming and orchard work, a wife Edith and two children, Vernon and Glenn, Daddy got the wanderlust. He bought a Model T Ford, and we headed north for Oregon and Washington. He worked his way there by working on farms and fixing broken-down cars along the way. After working on building grain elevators, the Columbia River highway, saw mills, and working in the woods as a lumberjack in Washington, the folks had seen enough of the Northwest, and we headed back to Southern California on the Southern Pacific Railroad. (I don't know what happened to the Model T Ford.) Brother Ralph was born in Portland, Oregon.

Sometime after coming back to California, Dad went to work for Mama's brother who owned a steam shovel and took jobs all over the state. We followed him through deserts, rivers, and wilderness, living in tents and camping out. During this time a new member of the family had arrived on the scene, Genevieve, making three boys and one girl.

After all the wandering in the wilderness, we had come back to Santa Monica where Daddy grew up as a boy. Marion Harris, Forrest's father had come across the plains on the Oregon trail as a small boy. He had migrated down the coast and became a cattleman with a spread in the Santa Monica Mountains, near Malibu where Forrest was born. Marion sold his ranch and moved to Santa Monica when Forrest was 12 years old.

The fifth child, Nellie May, was born in Santa Monica in 1923, and it looked like we had at last settled down for a long stay. Santa Monica was a beautiful city on the coast with nice streets, a harbor, and a business district. Daddy found plenty of work with his dump truck and taking out trees. We boys all had paper routes, and Momma was busy taking care of all of us. Our uncle, Dad's brother, had a house moving business and owned almost a whole block on busy Lincoln Boulevard. At the end of the street on the corner, he had a store building probably about 80 feet square. It had been a Fuller paint store in Ocean Park, and he had moved it onto his property. It had been rented at various times to different businesses. It had been a second hand store and at another time a plumbing shop. The proprietor had placed a water closet up over the door to advertise his wares. This seemed to be too much of a temptation for the younger generation at Halloween time. The next morning as people were driving down Lincoln Boulevard on their way to work, they saw this life-like dummy sitting above the door and looking down the street.

The building became vacant along in 1926. It wasn't too much to look at; it had large plate glass windows on both sides of the front door, but it was in need of paint on the sides of the building. A group of Foursquare people, with a young couple for Pastors, rented the building. They cleaned it all up and covered the windows with colored paper to look like stained glass. They bought a roll of burlap and divided the building in half; the front part became the sanctuary, and the back part was divided up for Sunday School rooms. They built a platform at the back of the sanctuary with a pulpit, and they had their little "church." These people were very devoted and dedicated; they canvassed the neighborhood getting people to come to their little church. They had a burning desire to see people come into a saving knowledge of Jesus Christ, and things were beginning to happen.

Aimee Semple McPherson, who had been traveling all over the land with great revival meetings, decided to settle down in Los Angeles. She built Angelus Temple and Life Bible College, and a host of people were being inspired, trained, and sent out to establish churches and to evangelize. It was like a piece of metal being heated red hot and laid on the anvil to beat into shape, with sparks flying in all directions. Churches were springing up all over Southern California, Goodyear, Glendale, Santa Monica, Burbank, San Diego, and on and on. The lady workers in the church all looked so nice in their white nurses uniforms with a big black tie and a white cross in the front.

And so the five Harris children were drawn in along with others to this new little church. We had been going to Sunday School at the big church in downtown Santa Monica. I won't say they didn't teach the salvation message, but, if they did, I somehow didn't seem to comprehend it. I was young and perhaps missed it, but it seems to me that what I got out of it was mostly a social gospel; that is, do the best you can, be honest and upright, and everything will come out alright in the end. But in this little store-front church we soon knew what the gospel was all about. After all these years, I still remember the Pastors' last name. It was Mendelson, but I don't remember their first names. They were a young couple, probably in their 20's, very zealous for the Lord, and very powerful in their preaching. They were both good preachers. All of us kids received the Lord as our Savior under their ministry. I remember the Sunday morning I went forward in 1927. I was 12 years old and under such conviction I felt like the weight of the world was on my shoulders. After kneeling at the altar, I poured my heart out to the Lord, and I felt such a release; I arose feeling light as a feather. That little old building looked like a cathedral; it was beautiful!

After we kids were saved, we couldn't rest until Momma and Daddy were brought into the church and saved. We kept after them until we got them into the church. Once they were in the little church, the Holy Spirit did His work, they were saved, and we were one happy family serving the Lord. A little while later, on an evening we drove to Los Angeles to Angelus Temple and were all baptized together as a family by Brother Arthur and Sister McPherson. Momma and Daddy were baptized together, and I don't know how they managed, as Daddy was 6 feet, 2 inches, and weighed 260 pounds. We three boys were baptized together and Genevieve alone. Many of our relatives were listening by radio to the baptismal service.

I remember on several occasions we drove up to Angelus Temple from Santa Monica. We drove up Santa Monica Boulevard to Sunset Boulevard and up Sunset to Glendale Boulevard to Angelus Temple. The world looked so beautiful in our new-found joy in the Lord. Angelus Temple was still in revival, and it was packed out every night of the week, with people singing all the old hymns with the joy of the Lord on their faces. It was a wonderful experience for us new babes in Christ. We were awestruck by the choir, the silver band, and the great throbbing organ. It seemed to all blend together into a symphony of praise to a God we all loved with all our hearts.

On the way home, everything took on new meaning and beauty, the big red Pacific Electric cars and the Los Angeles yellow street cars, the traffic with the many models and makes of cars, the pedestrians and shoppers wearing the fashions of the day, and the sky with the clouds turning to yellow and reds over the Santa Monica Mountains as the sun hung low in the western sky. Truly our hearts were bursting with a new joy that was beyond anything we could have ever imagined! We went back to our little store-front church with a new zeal to work and to do God's will. I remember taking my Bible to school and reading it at recess.

We boys were busy after school delivering papers on our paper routes. The Santa Monica Evening Outlook and the Los Angeles Express were brought down from Los Angeles every afternoon by truck. We opened our two bundles of papers; the Express was slipped inside the Outlook, and the two were boxed together and put into bags on the back of our bikes to be thrown out to our customers as we went down the street. I remember that we used to slip a tract into each paper as we folded them together. I don't know if it was legal or not, but I guess at our young age we didn't know much about the "legal" business.

Well, a couple of years went by and Daddy's feet were getting itchy again; he decided to homestead on the Mojave Desert, near a little town called Muroc, next to a big dry lake. The nearest Foursquare Church was 30 miles away in Lancaster, California. We went a few times, but the 60-mile round trip was too much for our old car with its poor tires, so we had to quit going. Before long we had all sort of backslid. God hadn't forgotten us, and he sent us a man that loved the Lord with his whole heart and loved to preach His Word. Seneca Lowell Griggs was a layman with a family. He was a poor working man with a five-day-a-week job, no car, and very little money, but when he found this little band of people in Muroc hungry to hear the Word preached, he made the 200-mile round trip to minister to us each Sunday at the one-room school in Muroc. Sometimes a friend would bring him up; other times if he had a little money, he would take the Southern Pacific to Lancaster and hitchhike out to Muroc. If he was short of money, he would hitchhike all the way from Los Angeles and witness to everyone who gave him a ride. He was really a dedicated man of God.

The Robert Steward family had moved to Randsburg, California, when Bob had taken a mining job at the Yellow Aster Gold Mine. They had heard about our family through some friends who had also moved up there. They came down to visit, and we became friends and visited back and forth some. Leita Mae came down and preached for us a time or two. One time, the three Steward girls happened to be down when Bro. Griggs was there. When he saw those three girls, his eyes popped out and he said, "Wow! If I was 35 years younger and single, I would set my cap for one of those beautiful Christian girls!" I was going steady by this time with a wonderful Christian girl, but I guess Glenn took the hint because the next thing we knew, Glenn and Roberta were dating. Later, they had a beautiful wedding in the Randsburg District Foursquare Church.

As time raced by, all seven children married and raised families. Momma and Daddy had added two more daughters, Patricia and Darleene, to the family and we became a great Christian congregation of our own from sea to shining sea and from border to border. Our family can be found all over the U.S.A.

and parts of Canada, from Canada to the great plains of Texas, and from the Pacific Ocean to Baltimore, Maryland on the Atlantic.

In this family, there are seven pastors, two medical doctors, two nurses, three school teachers, a university professor, four engineers, several PhD's, 16 attended Bible College; there are many college graduates and some still in college, there are entrepreneurs and successful business people. There are now around 140 people, not counting a brother and sister and several nieces and nephews who have gone on ahead to see our Savior and enjoy the beauties of heaven with Momma and Daddy.

I could tell many wonderful stories about this family, but I have left out most names and personalities because the theme of this story is about the dedicated Christians that brought the original seven of this family to a saving knowledge of Jesus the Savior.

Perhaps these young Christians, fresh out of Bible school were a little awed by the beautiful churches in town and a little embarrassed by their little old store building, but revival fires were burning, and they felt the love of God in their hearts and the power of the Holy Spirit in their message—a tent or a cottage, they didn't care; they were building for eternity over there.

This is the story of just one family in that little church. How many other families were started on the right road because of that faithful little band, only our Lord knows. What a blessing it's been to all of us!

Week 1

Songs in the Night

by Aleta Phelps
Niece to Glenn Harris

*"Tell your children about it,
Let your children tell their children,
And their children another **generation**."
Joel 1:3 NKJV*

Mind is racing, trying to figure it all out... The Lord brings songs in the night.

Psalm 42:8 "... and in the night His song shall be with me..."

Lord, this is not going where I thought we would be or what I thought we would have to go through...

"'Cause even in the madness there is peace... Through all of this chaos You are writing a symphony, a symphony..." — *Symphony*

Lord, help me not despise but embrace what You are changing in me.

2 Chronicles 20:3 "Jehoshaphat didn't know what to do but... resolved that he should inquire of the Lord."

Rest. God will fight our battles as we fight our battles in worship and surrender.

"... So my weapons are praise and thanksgiving ... and I will lift my song of praise for what You've done. This is how I fight my battles (repeat) It may look like I'm surrounded but I'm surrounded by You (repeat)." Upper Room — *Surrounded*

Lord, help us to teach each generation of Your faithfulness; to be bold and courageous.

"I am created by God. He designed me so I am not a mistake. His son died for me. Just so I could be forgiven. He picked me to be His own, so I am chosen. He redeemed me so I am wanted. He showed me grace just so I could be saved. He has a future for me because He loves me. So I don't wonder any more. I am a child of God." Overcomer — *Ask Me Who I Am*

Week 2

God is Good

by Debbie West Jones and Sherri West Coats
Granddaughters of Glenn Harris

*For the Lord is good and his love endures forever; his faithfulness continues through all **generations**. Psalm 100:5 NIV*

Our mother, Marilyn Harris West, believed this verse to her core and taught her four children to always look for the good in every situation. Our mom was an incredible listener and so wise in her counsel to us. She always took the time to help us reframe every hardship and difficulty we faced as an opportunity to see how good God was and how He was always there for us. In fact, looking back, we see that our mom was sort of a picture of what our Heavenly Father is to us. Sometimes we would call mom on the phone and ask if she was busy. Her answer was always, "Never too busy for you." I think that is the same response God must have for us.

In 1991, as we stood from a distance watching her home burn, our mom turned to us and excitedly said, "I can't wait to see what good God is going to bring from this!" Wow!! What a life lesson for us all. The statement she made on that difficult day is testimony to her belief that God is good, that his love endures forever, and that his faithfulness continues to all generations!

In 1994, our mom and dad were killed by a drunk driver. We struggled to find the good, but we knew through years of her teaching, counseling, and example that God was good and that his love and faithfulness were forever. Now, twenty-five years later, we believe this verse to our core and continue to look for God's goodness in all things and pointing out God's goodness to the generations that follow us.

Father, teach us that You are good, no matter our circumstances. Amen.

Week 3

Knowing Jesus

by Asher Lambert, 10, and Gideon Lambert, 6
Grandsons of Lolita Frederick Harris,
the daughter-in-law of Vern Harris

"If they say this, our descendants can reply, 'Look at this copy of the LORD's altar that our ancestors made. It is not for burnt offerings or sacrifices; it is a reminder of the relationship both of us have with the LORD.'" Joshua 22:28 NLT

We both know Jesus and have accepted Him as our Lord and Savior and have asked Him to live in our hearts forever. We accepted Him by saying a prayer with our mom and dad, and that was pretty special! We were thinking about how most people, if they were born in a family that didn't serve Jesus, might not get to know Him. Some people come to know Him through friends at school, and then they get to know another Christian family.

We're so thankful that we have kids in our world that we can tell about Jesus and help them get to know Him, accept Him into their hearts, and get connected to a good church. But most of all, we are thankful that we get to grow up in a family that knows and serves Jesus; back to our great, great, great-grandparents. We want our great, great, great, great-grandchildren to know Jesus too, so we will be sure to tell our kids and grandkids about Him. You should too!

Week 4

by Darleene Harris Hemmerling
Daughter of Forrest and Edith Harris

Now Generation:

> *"Choose you this day whom you will serve... As for me and my house we will serve the Lord." Joshua 24:15b,d KJV*

Future Generations:

> *Blessed is the man who fears the Lord, who delights greatly in His commandments. His descendants will be mighty. The **generations** of the upright will be blessed. Psalm 112:1-2 NKJV*

We all must make a choice, a decision. The choice we make will not only profit us individually, but our children and all the generations in the future. We cannot make the decision for our children, but we can teach them and bring them up in a manner that they will witness the love of God and choose Jesus to be their own savior.

The story of our family's spiritual journey has always been an inspiration to me. Way before I was born, when dad and mom had the first five children, they dropped off the older children at a fancy church in Santa Monica where they did not hear the salvation message. Then a storefront church opened with a pastor and congregation really on fire for the Lord. My oldest brother Vernon was the first in the family to make the decision to accept Jesus as Savior. Vern, in his written stories, takes no credit for bringing the rest of the family to the Lord. However, I remember how my mother told the story. She said after Vern accepted the Lord, he would not be satisfied until his brothers (age 10 & 8) and sister (age 6) came to the same decision. Before long the whole family believed.

We, who have benefitted from the great choices our previous generations have made, must start where they did and make our own great choices so that we bless the generations who follow us. I pray each of us do just that.

P.S. For the many children's workers in the family, this story should highlight the value of one child you bring to a saving knowledge of Jesus Christ.

Week 5

A Greater Mission

by Jodi Pullen Coats
Great-granddaughter-in-law of Glenn Harris

*We will not hide them from their descendants; we will tell the next **generation** the praiseworthy deeds of the Lord, his power, and the wonders he has done.*
Psalm 78:4 NIV

In 2016, Wes and I had the pleasure of visiting France as Wes's college graduation trip. We were able to visit Notre Dame Cathedral and Basilica of the Sacred Heart of Paris. These cathedrals were unlike anything I've ever seen. I couldn't help but cry as we sat in the pews. We learned that Notre Dame took 200 years to construct and Basilica of the Sacred Heart took almost 50 years to construct. It's amazing to think that some people spent their whole lives building something that they never got to see complete, but kept working in service to a greater mission than themselves. They knew that the next generation would continue work they had started and that what they were building was bigger than any one person or generation. They were spending their time and resources building something that would last far past their own personal influence.

Is my time being used to work in service to a greater mission than myself? What am I building today that will last? These are questions that I need to ask myself every day. As life gets busy, I hope we can remember daily, that we are responsible for building something bigger than ourselves. Let us remember today to "tell the next generation the praiseworthy deeds of the Lord, his power, and the wonders he has done."

Week 6

Everyone has Something

by Katelyn Jones Truett
Great-granddaughter of Glenn Harris

"And afterward, I will pour out my Spirit on all people. Your sons and daughters will prophesy, your old men will dream dreams, your young men will see visions. Even on my servants, both men and women, I will pour out my Spirit in those days."
Joel 2:28-29 NIV

We live in a time when division is seen in almost every arena. Gender, race, political stance, religion. . . There is division in all of it. Unfortunately, generations are not exempt from this. Older generations feel that young people are lazy and entitled, while young people complain that the generations before them lack flexibility and creativity.

The reality is that one of the most powerful and effective ways to bring unity is to be in tune with the Holy Spirit. When we read Scriptures like the one above, we must pause to recognize the unification of generations—"sons and daughters," "young men and old men". We all have a part to play; we have all been given a piece of the puzzle.

We would be wise to look around ourselves to see who is represented in our circles. Do you see "old men" and "young men" (not gender specific, obviously)? If not, start there! Begin spending time with people older and younger than you. Be open and willing to see what the Holy Spirit has given them (their piece of the puzzle) as a valuable contribution. In the Kingdom of God, everyone has value; everyone brings something to the table. If you only surround yourself with people in your generation, the puzzle will be incomplete. Make sure you glean from those who have gone before you, and those who are coming behind you because, according to this Scripture, God is pouring out His Spirit on them.

Week 7

Faith Runners

by Josh Harris and Ethan Harris
Grandsons of Ralph Harris

Therefore, since we are surrounded by such a great cloud of witnesses, let us throw off everything that hinders and the sin that so easily entangles. And let us run with perseverance the race marked out for us. Hebrews 12:1 NIV

"Do what your heart tells you." "You deserve it." "You just need to make sure you are looking out for yourself first. Self-care, you know." "No one else can tell you what's best for you."

We live in a culture that is radically individualistic. We are told that we are the masters of our own lives, that we are the measure and the means of our own success. No one else can tell us what to do or that our actions or feelings are wrong. But at the end of the day, this intense commitment to individual freedom leaves us utterly alone. The illusion that personal happiness is the highest aim eventually subsides and leaves us feeling empty. We are left with no purpose and no support.

Thankfully, Scripture gives us a very different vision of how our lives ought to be led. The writer of Hebrews tells us, "Therefore, since we are surrounded by such a great cloud of witnesses, let us throw off everything that hinders and the sin that so easily entangles. And let us run with perseverance the race marked out for us" (Heb. 12:1). This passage comes immediately after the "hall of faith" chapter, in which the great heroes of the Old Testament are recognized for their steady obedience to God in the face of arduous trials and yet-to-be-fulfilled promises. We are encouraged to draw inspiration from the generations of believers that have come before us and shown us what it looks like to run the race well. In our family, we have even had the privilege of watching some world-class faith-runners in action before our eyes.

It is also worth noting the use of the plural "us" in the verse. This race is not an individual event. We are not only "surrounded by a cloud of witnesses" but joined by a crowd of teammates pushing toward the same end, all called to "throw off" the chains of sin and put on the mantle of endurance. Rather than being bound by our fruitless search for individual accolades and fulfillment, we can find faith, hope, and love in the example of previous generations, the encouragement of our fellow runners, and most of all in the call of our glorious savior. Let's run this race!

Week 8

The Entire Generation

by Charlotte Epperson Harris
Daughter-in-law of Glenn Harris

*How joyful are those who fear the Lord and delight in obeying his commands. Their children will be successful everywhere; an entire **generation** of godly people will be blessed. Psalm 112:1-2 NIV*

... And I will tell everyone about the wonderful things you do. Psalm 73:28 NLT

In Psalm 112, there is a description of people who fear the Lord and obey His commands. The promise is that an entire generation will be blessed. I have personally been a witness to that blessing that was passed on to a generation. I have been a witness to healing, provision, joy, protection. I have observed a family generous, compassionate, a family that conducts their business fairly. Verse six even says that they will be long remembered.

After pondering Psalm 112, in a non-related chapter, I read this verse that really struck me: Psalm 73:28 "And I will tell about the wonderful things you do."

I suddenly realized that I have not been faithful to testify to this generation of God's faithfulness to us on this "life's journey". I remember Glenn and Roberta sharing with us many of their miracles. We all need to remember to pass along to the next generation the miracles in our lives.

Week 9

God's Faithfulness

by Kimberly Ann Harris Ricigliano
Granddaughter of Vern Harris

*For the Lord is good and his love endures forever; his faithfulness continues through all **generations**. Psalm 100:5 NIV*

God's faithfulness has continued over the past five generations in my family. My great grandparents, Forrest and Edith Harris, became Christians because of my grandfather, Vern Harris. The faithfulness of God to lead a Sunday School teacher to share the gospel with Vern led generations of Harris families to become Christians. Vern was said to have nine lives as he had nine near death experiences.

My dad, Paul Harris, grew up watching the "flying wing" fly over his home. The flying wing was considered a failure, so years later when he was led to work for Northrop as project manager building the factory of the future for aircraft modeled after the flying wing, he thought Lord this cannot be right. But God was faithful as he had a great career building a factory of the future.

When I was a single mom with a single income, I really came to trust in God's provision and faithfulness. A company I worked for closed suddenly and God provided for me and my daughter. My daughter, Shannan Andersen, felt Vanguard college was where she was to go, but tuition was expensive. I told her if she feels that is where God wants her then He will be faithful and provide. By the time she graduated, her college tuition was paid off.

God's faithfulness endures throughout all generations. He will never revoke it or alter things one generation to the next. As previous generations have found Him faithful, so will our future generations. His word is truth. True to His word, He gave His only son to die for our sins. Praise God for His faithfulness!

Our Father, who art in Heaven, thank You for Your goodness, love (mercy), and faithfulness (truth) from generation to generation. Help us to know that even though each generation may face its challenges and tragedies, You remain faithful to work all things for good for those who love You. And in the end, we'll come to understand and see the results of passing on Your truth from generation to generation. In Jesus' name, Amen.

Week 10

The Character of God

by Ashley Duncan West
Great-granddaughter-in-law of Glenn Harris

*"Understand, therefore, that the Lord your God is indeed God. He is the faithful God who keeps his covenant for a thousand **generations** and lavishes his unfailing love on those who love him and obey his commands." Deuteronomy 7:9 NLT*

This verse is Moses speaking to the Israelites before they get to enter the promised land. They have been in the wilderness for 40 years, wandering. This is the last message that He gets to deliver from God. And it is such a powerful one. I feel like this single verse speaks so much of the character of God. There are several things we can pull from this verse about God.

1. God is faithful. He is loyal, constant, and steadfast. In a world where things change day by day, God is always the same, always on our side, and always near to us.

2. God values relationship. A covenant is a promise, an agreement. But, it is also a relationship. A relationship that has rules that are not meant to be broken without consequences. God extends this covenant to us, to have relationship with us.

3. God is eternal. Not only does He keep His covenants, His promises, but, He keeps them for a thousand generations! This means His promise doesn't just apply to you, or your children, or even your grandchildren, but ONE THOUSAND GENERATIONS!

4. God's love never fails. All people fail at some point. But, God never fails us. His love is always for us, when life or people fail us, when we fail others, even when we fail Him.

Week 11

Flowing like Water

by Leahna Frederick West
Granddaughter-in-law of Glenn Harris

*Your faithfulness flows from one **generation** to the next, all that you created sits firmly in place to testify of you. Psalm 119:90 TPT*

There is something about nature that moves me: a sunrise or sunset, a beautiful flower, a stately tree... It speaks to me of God's creativity; it proves that He wants to share His love for us through His artistry. It is soothing to me to think that a loved one who passed may have enjoyed looking at the same intricate tree, that one who lives far away might be noticing the same star, or that in the future, one will appreciate the same majestic scenery I did.

One of the most calming aspects of nature for me is water, the waves of the ocean, ripples in a pond, or gurgling of a stream; there is just a sense of peace and tranquility they bring me. With water, there is constant, steady movement.

God's love for us is the same. He pours it out continuously, steadily, always. All we have to do is accept it and step into it. Look for evidence of this love in your own life. You will find it in the past, present, and even the future! Share with others how He loves and blesses you, your family, and your friends. Tell about His grace and mercy that is new every morning! And if you need a reminder of His faithful, unfailing love, step outside and go take a walk, enjoying nature!

Week 12

Early Impressions

by Patricia Harris Kauffman
Daughter of Forrest and Edith Harris

*We will not hide them from their children, Telling to the next **generation** to come the praises of the Lord, And His strength and His wonderful works that He has done. Psalm 78:4 NKJV*

When I was still three years old (I may have been almost four), I witnessed something that left an indelible impression on me. That impression is still with me to this day. I was sitting next to my mother in the little rock chapel in Victorville, California. It was prayer time. I observed my mother, Edith Evelyn Harris, worshipping the Lord with all her heart. Her arms were slightly raised, her hands cupped in a receiving mode, and she shook with some intensity (not because she was old or weak. She was a strong woman). I could tell she was talking, but not audibly. She was totally oblivious to anything going on around her. Her expression was humble but intensely on Him, whom she so adored.

That image stuck with me. It is a picture of my mother's life of devotion to the Lord Jesus. She grabbed that moment when she could forget the farm work at home and concentrate on her Lord. It told me how dearly she truly loved Him and how much He meant to her.

My word to young parents raising children is to let your children observe you deeply engaged in worship. It will say more to them than words.

Week 13

Seek God's Will

by Matthew Tamashiro-Harris
Great-grandson of Glenn Harris

*No one remembers the former **generations**,
and even those yet to come will not be remembered
by those who follow them.*
Ecclesiastes 1:11 NIV

Our life on earth is only temporary; someday, we will all pass on from this life and eventually fade from memory, given enough time. That might sound sad, but also notice that this means all of your regrets and all of your embarrassing moments won't be remembered. So live your life boldly, unafraid of what anyone else will think of you because in the end none of their opinions will matter. Likewise, don't waste time comparing yourself to others, thinking that your life should be a certain way or that you should have certain material possessions just because other people do. Eventually, none of that will make a difference.

At the end of Ecclesiastes, the Preacher, who wrote it, delivers his final conclusion after pondering the meaninglessness of life. He says that ultimately what matters is to follow God and his commandments. In the end, our earthly life is temporary, but God is forever; His opinions will never fade. Therefore, don't chase the opinions of the mortal humans around you, but seek God's will. That is the way to success in this life.

Week 14

Impacting Generations

by Lori Coats Pirtle
Great-granddaughter of Glenn Harris

*"And his mercy is for those who fear him from **generation** to **generation**." Luke 1:50 ESV*

As a mother, I often consider how Mary felt being the mother of Jesus. Luke 1:46-56 gives insight to her heart while she was pregnant with the Son of God. Mary's humble song of praise shows how genuinely blessed she felt to be chosen for such a major role. She's not begging to be released of her duty and she doesn't elevate herself above others because she was chosen as Jesus' mother.

We can all see how important Mary's role was in the coming of Christ but what about the people who taught Mary to open her heart to the Lord? They're not spotlighted in the nativity but their roles were just as important. Mary understood the importance of passing her faith through the generations because she was likely a product of this practice.

We won't all have a heavily spotlighted role, like being the mother of Jesus. But passing his mercy to future generations can impact the world in ways we could never imagine.

So, if you're feeling mundane in parenthood, remember the importance of the work you're doing. It may seem insignificant today, but the impact it will have on future generations is limitless.

Week 15

Spiritual Inheritance

by Joy Harris Grady
Daughter of Vern Harris

*Lord, through all **generations** thou has been our dwelling place. Psalm 90:1*

In one of my gardens, I made a memorial for my mother, Thelma Harris. I had this very verse engraved in brass and installed for all to see. As a child, I was fortunate enough to hear my great-grandmother testify to her faith in God. From, early on, I knew our family belonged to the Lord.

In Proverbs 13:22, it says, "A good person leaves an inheritance for their children's children..." As I look around my home, I see things I inherited from my mom and dad and grandparents. These things have great sentimental value and elicit precious memories, but the greatest thing I inherited from my parents was being brought up in a Christian home. Because of the spiritual inheritance my parents modeled for me, I committed my life to the Lord at a young age.

My great-grandparents, grandparents, parents, brothers, aunts, uncles, and cousins have all contributed to my growth as a Christian. I am thrilled as I see my children and grandchildren walk with the Lord; I know they are passing on the Christian faith to their children. As I think back over previous Ada Connections, many of our family have gone to be with the Lord. They were part of my spiritual inheritance, and I will always be grateful for them.

What a great inheritance!

Week 16

The Impact of Faith

by Savannah Jones Daniel
Great-granddaughter of Glenn Harris

*"You are blessed because you believed that the Lord would do what he said." Mary responded, "Oh, how my soul praises the Lord. For he took notice of his lowly servant girl, and from now on all **generations** will call me blessed." Luke 1:45-46, 48 NLT*

Mary was not previously known worldwide and had no desire to be known this way. The Lord took her humble and faithful heart and molded it into what He called her to be. Mary had incredible faith that what she had been told about the Messiah being born to her was complete truth. Because Mary believed and was faithful, generations have talked about her and have come to believe in Jesus.

The faith and resilience of our parents, grandparents, great grandparents, and beyond has impacted our family and brought us to where we are today.

Our own faith in Jesus can and will impact generations to come, but we have to claim that faith as our own. We can't live off the faith of our family members. The Lord has called each of us to something incredible.

Take hold and proclaim to those around you what the Lord has done.

Week 17

Sharing with Others

by Kathy Pinson
Friend of the Glenn Harris family

*Let this be recorded for future **generations**,
so that a people not yet born will praise the LORD.
Psalm 102:18 NLT*

I can't help but smile and feel my spirit lift any time I see a picture of my family. The pictures bring good memories of who they are and of the times we've spent together and the memories made. But, unless those pictures and memories are shared with others, they will soon be lost. Many times I sat with my mother or other members of her generation as pictures were shared of earlier generations. Inevitably stories of who those individuals were, or memories made with them, are told. As they are told, I hear of the legacy of those individuals.

As I view pictures of my mother and father today, I am reminded again of who they were, of their incredible love for me and all the wonderful times we shared.

So it is with the nature of God and His marvelous works for us. We need to tell of the wonders and greatness of God to our generation and the generations following us.

I read a devotional recently which asked the question, "Why are these stories of Jesus recorded in the Bible?" The answer was, "Not to tell us what Jesus did, but, rather, to tell us what He does." Knowing the love, nature, and power of our God is necessary to build our faith and to have hope in this life and the life to come.

Week 18

Grace to Obey

by Margie Debord Lundie
Daughter of Genevieve Harris Debord Blenkhorn

*"For I the Lord thy God am a jealous God, visiting the iniquity of the fathers upon the children unto the third and fourth **generation** of them that hate me; and showing mercy unto thousands of them that love me and keep my commandments."*
Exodus 20:5-6 KJV

Although at first glance this verse of warning seems ominous, it is a very comforting message. God reminds the Israelites that He delivered them from Egyptian slavery, giving them wealth, direction, victory over enemies, healing, sustenance, shoes and clothes. Besides physical needs He gave principles of successful conduct: complete religious, legal, nutritional-medicinal systems. He provided EVERYTHING!

He is the blessed provider of all things. None other can supply your needs, and particularly not by your own actions. If you have a need and attempt to fulfill it through the control and manipulation of situations and people—instead of trusting God as your provider—you are demonstrating to the Lord your lack of faith and modeling for your children conduct that God forbids but behaviors they may mimic. In this way, your faithlessness is visited upon your children. This is a significant aspect of the treachery of idolatry. Instead of human effort, trust God to provide completely.

Oh, the blessed relief of not having to work and strain, worry and stress. He does it all! Even our faith and salvation. To protect the generations to come, we only need use the grace He gives to love Him by obeying Him. Comfort indeed, rest in Him.

Week 19

Spread the Good News

by Vickie Ragsdale
Family friend of Glenn and Ralph Harris

*One **generation** will commend your works to another; they will tell of your mighty acts. Psalm 145:4 NIV*

There was a knock on our apartment door. We opened it to find Ruth (Terry's mom) holding bags of groceries. She explained that the store was offering double Blue Chip stamps and that after selecting her groceries, she still didn't have enough to redeem them for the item she'd been saving for. So, her solution was to buy more groceries — for us.

Terry and I smiled because Ruth didn't know we'd paid our tithe and paid our bills, but didn't have money left for groceries. Ruth wasn't just buying groceries so she could get something she wanted, she was buying groceries because God used her 'want' to supply our 'need'. (By the way, the variety of food she chose was exactly what we needed.)

When we recognize the Lord's everyday provisions, and reflect on the testimonies from our own experiences or those passed on from our parents, grandparents, and great-grandparents, our faith is increased. And when we remember Bible 'stories' we learned from Sunday School, Vacation Bible School, church camp, Bible studies and sermons of God's mighty acts, our faith is strengthened. So, continue to have those conversations about bags of groceries or surviving a tornado or being healed or your many blessings. Tell others about how good God is, how much God loves us, and what God has done for you.

Spread the Good News.

Week 20

Be Intentional

by Mark Harris
Son of Vern Harris

*After that whole **generation** had gathered to their fathers, another **generation** grew up, who knew neither the Lord nor what He had done for Israel.*
Judges 2:10 NIV

Joshua and the generation of Israelites, who had experienced the miraculous victories of taking possession of their land of promise, had passed away and somehow had failed to sufficiently pass along their knowledge of the Lord's love and the experience of His miraculous provision to the next generation. Perhaps they were so busy fighting battles and setting up communities to make a better future for their children that they thought their children would automatically make the connection. Whatever the reason for their failure, the next generation forsook the Lord and worshiped false gods.

Our family has a tremendous spiritual heritage. Over 90 years ago, Forrest and Edith Harris and their five children (Pat and Darleene weren't born yet) were baptized at Angelus Temple, expressing their faith in Christ. Through the years, our family members have served the Lord in various capacities and in various parts of the world experiencing many miraculous blessings and victories in possessing God's land of promise.

It behooves us to make sure that our children, grandchildren, and great grandchildren experience the same intimate relationship with Jesus and the same miraculous victories in their walk with Him. Pray for them regularly, share with them your own stories, teach them your values, and show them God's love and acceptance. Don't expect that it will just happen automatically.

What a tragedy for the generation of Israelites following one of the greatest supernatural experiences in Israel's history to have lost their personal relationship with the Lord and the joy of experiencing His miraculous power and provision. May it not be so of our future generations.

Week 21

Recipe for Blessing

by Robyn Wisler Harris
Daughter-in-law of Vern Harris

*What we have heard and known, what our fathers have told us, we will not hide them from our children; we will tell the next **generation** the praiseworthy deeds of the Lord, His power, and the wonders He has done. Psalm 78:3-4, paraphrased*

In my family, we have recipes that have been handed down from my mother and other family members that we serve on special occasions for our family and friends. It's always a delight to enjoy these special dishes and the memories they rekindle. And now, with my girls all married with their own families, it is fun to see them serving some of those family dishes on their special occasions, as well.

Likewise, there is no greater joy than to see my girls and their families serving the Lord with dedication and enthusiasm soundly anchored in the foundations of faith that have been passed on from generation to generation.

In the Psalmist's day, family oral traditions were one of the primary vehicles of passing on the knowledge and understanding of the power and goodness of God. Even in my own growing up years, before the distractions of television and iPhones, I remember sitting around the kitchen table as my parents, grandparents, aunts and uncle would reminisce and tell stories of things that happened through the years. Many of those stories had great spiritual lessons that helped shape my life and values.

Your stories of God's faithfulness and power are spiritual recipes that will bless generations to come and will help shape lives in a solid foundation of faith in Christ.

Week 22

Generations

by Melvin Harris
Son of Glenn Harris

*But you are a chosen **generation**, a royal priesthood, a holy nation. His own special people, that you may proclaim the praises of him who called you out of darkness into his marvelous light... 1 Peter 2:9 NLT*

God loves people and he loves generations! Through the ages, God has pronounced blessings on people and on generations, and in some instances, he has pronounced judgment on people and generations. One notable man, on whom God pronounced blessings, was Abraham. In reviewing Abraham's story, I realized that not all of Abraham's descendants lived in the blessing that God promised them. It seemed that some wanted to live their own way. I have had the wonderful privilege of being a part of the Forrest Harris "Blessed Generations"! It is amazing to see God pour out his blessing on us. I don't ever want to get out from under that blessing. I desire to live according to God's way!

In 1 Peter 2:9, Peter reminds the church of God's amazing "PROMISE" that we are a special "Generation". What a wonderful salvation Christ's death provided for each and every one of us. Wow! A promise that even exceeds the blessings that God pronounces on generations. Makes me want to live a life pleasing to him and proclaim his praises to the world!

Week 23

Unfailing Love

by Brittany West
Great-granddaughter of Glenn Harris

*For the Lord is good. His unfailing love continues forever, and his faithfulness continues to each **generation**. Psalm 100:5 NLT*

How would your life change if you lived every day knowing these truths and thinking about them constantly? Knowing time, circumstances, or people cannot change God's character; He is always faithful, His love is unfailing, and He is always good. This promise is true for every generation!

Personally, this changes my perspective, eliminates worry, and brings immense joy! I can trust His plans for me and for those I love are always the best because He loves with an endless, unfailing love. This assurance is meant to be imparted to both our families and other families. God has gripped my heart to not only speak of His goodness, love, and faithfulness but to live in it. I want my life to display steadfast trust in who He is.

The preceding context of this verse is a call to live in thanksgiving and with a heart of worship. If we thank Him daily for who He is and for His blessings, constantly glorifying His name, we will sincerely know in the depths of our hearts that He is good, loving, and faithful.

Father, thank You for who You are. Thank You for choosing to love us and for sending Jesus so we can know You intimately. Help us to live in Your promises and to share them through our words and actions. In Jesus' name, amen.

Week 24

A Parent's Influence

by Patricia Harris Kauffman
Daughter of Forrest and Edith Harris

*... They should make them known to their children; that the **generation** to come might know... that they may set their hope in God, and not forget the works of God. Psalm 78:5-7 NKJV*

I remember many times in winter around home when my mother would share things she had learned or experienced in life. She had grown older in those days and gleaned much wisdom. I wish I could remember specific things to share with you, but my memory fails me. They did have a big impact on my future life.

She was a hard working woman out in the field alongside my dad in the summer, but in the winter she spent more time around the house. She probably wasn't sure I was taking it to heart, but I was. I wasn't much of a talker—I think I am high-functioning autistic—but I was a good listener. I'm so thankful she passed it on to me. I learned so many valuable things from my mom.

You may not think your children and grandchildren are listening or that what you say will make much of an impression on them, but I think you will be surprised. When you talk to them about what you have learned from your experiences, especially about how it relates to the Lord, it will have meaning.

I think perhaps parents and kids are too busy and involved in too many activities to find time to talk or listen. Maybe you need to consciously set aside time. This can have far-reaching spiritual consequences or rewards.

Week 25

Legacy of Faith

by Michele Hemmerling Isaac
Daughter of Darleene Harris Hemmerling

*Do all things without grumbling or disputing; so that you will prove yourselves to be blameless and innocent, children of God above reproach in the midst of a crooked and perverse **generation**, among whom you appear as lights in the world, holding fast the word of life, so that in the day of Christ I will have reason to glory because I did not run in vain nor toil in vain. Philippians 2:14-16 NASB*

My favorite faith story is the story of Uncle Vern attending the little Sunday school in a former plumbing shop with a toilet over the door. The couple running that Sunday School were faithful to the call and changed our family. I am so thankful that they spoke the truth and that Uncle Vern's heart was changed. He took that good news home to his family. Each family member made a personal decision to follow Jesus. It is the legacy of faith our family now has. We have a blessed heritage of faith but yet faith still remains a personal choice. Will we choose to yield our heart to Christ everyday like Uncle Vern did all those years ago? Will we choose to follow Jesus like the generations before us?

We need to actively be the light in this perverse generation. We need to hold fast to the word of life just as Uncle Vern and his sisters and brothers did in their generation. Just as Paul was cheering on the Philippians, I see my aunts and uncles cheering us to press on until the day of Christ. The blessing of a Godly family is our legacy, but FAITH is not a generational gift but an individual choice.

Lord, help me to be a beacon of light in this generation and help me to actively pass on a faith legacy to the next generation!

Week 26

Trust and Be Thankful

by Beverly Bates
Niece to Vern Harris

I pray that out of his glorious riches he may strengthen you with power through his Spirit in your inner being, so that Christ may dwell in your hearts through faith. And I pray that you being rooted and established in love, may have power, together with all the saints, to grasp how wide and long and high and deep is the love of Christ and to know this love that surpasses knowledge—that you may be filled to the measure of all the fullness of God.
Ephesians 3:16-19 NIV

We are so busy running here and running there, sometimes we need to just stop and listen to the things God has for us. If we stop and take the time to enter into His presence, we can feel His love reaching out to calm us and give us peace and strength. We can trust and be thankful that He will get us through the day.

By trusting Him, we can stop worrying and stressing. One of life's biggest struggles is worrying about tomorrow. All through each day, we can be thankful. Being thankful keeps us from criticizing and complaining about our daily irritations.

The world is not perfect; there will always be imperfections while we are here in this temporary home. We need to focus on today, trust and be thankful, and share these gifts of love, peace, and strength with our family for generations to come.

Week 27

Old and Gray

by Lolita Gurney Frederick Harris
Daughter-in-law of Vern Harris
and generational friend of the Glenn Harris Family

*Even when I am old and gray, do not forsake me, my God, till I declare your power to the next **generation**, your mighty acts to all who are to come. Psalm 71:18 NIV*

I discovered early as a mother that the best way to reflect the Lord to the next generation was by living my testimony before them and praying for them. As the next generations came along, it was a bit harder for them to watch my life due to distances, but I could still pray for them.

A rabbi once stated he believed God's blessings over Israel were in direct relation to Jewish parents blessing their children. As each baby came along, I would hold and rock them, and found it was the perfect time to pray over them and bless them. I can no longer hold them, but I continue to pray they will become the person God desires them to be. Now I don't live close to any of them, but I daily mention their names before the Throne and take special time on their birthdays and anniversaries to pray for them. We can expect God to do great and wonderful things down through our generations as we faithfully pray for them.

Now . . . I am old and gray! But my work is not over—I still pray that each generation that follows me may know His blessings, strength, and power. I have determined to live until I die, never wasting a day to bless those I love, trusting they can see Him in me and will be faithful until the day they are each called home. I pray you make this same determination.

Week 28

Renown of the Lord

by Dylan West
Great-grandson of Glenn Harris

*But you, Lord, sit enthroned forever; your renown endures through all **generations**. Psalm 102:12 NIV*

With a location firmly within the "Bible belt," growing up in Ada, Oklahoma meant that church played a role in your life regardless of religious status. Sadly, the number of individuals who professed Christ with their lips yet denied Him with their lives were as plentiful as the churches found on every corner.

Why does this occur? If the Lord's renown endures through all generations, why do new prodigals appear every day? I believe this is not a fault of God, but a fault of family. Christianity for many families is a social norm or requirement. However, this results in Christianity, and thus God, becoming nothing more than a duty to fill and a box to check. Obligation speaks nothing of the Lord's renown. The Hebrew word for renown translates into a memento, recollection, or commemoration. Conspicuously absent are the words duty, requirement, or obligation.

Going to church out of a sense of obligation is not a commemoration of the Lord. It is, at best, a tradition. It is the renown of the Lord, not tradition, that passes from generation to generation. The blessings our family has received over the years are too numerous to count and well known to us all. As we teach each generation of God's blessing, it is His renown, rather than an obligation, that endures.

For our family, Christianity is not a family tradition. Instead, the greatness of God is a family experience. Let us continue then to commemorate God's mighty blessings to each generation.

Week 29

The Turning Point

by Paul Kauffman
Son of Patricia Harris Kauffman

Praise the Lord.
Blessed is the man who fears the Lord,
who finds great delight in His commands.
His children will be mighty in the land;
*the **generation** of the upright will be blessed.*
Psalm 112: 1 – 2 NIV

The oldest generation of Harrises I can remember are my grandparents Forrest and Edith. I consider them "Generation One" since that's where it starts for me. There are a lot of generations prior to that, but I didn't know them personally. My mother Patricia is from "Gen Two", along with her 3 brothers and 3 sisters. The family size explodes in my generation, "Gen Three" where I have a brother and 19 cousins. Now our family is adding to the numbers with "Gen Six"!

Reading family history, I learned that my grandparents grew up in a Christian home, but drifted away from fellowship as young adults. Their children were often dropped off for Sunday school. The Holy Spirit moved on a young Vern Harris, and he accepted the Lord as a 12 year old. His brothers and sisters were soon saved as well, and the whole family started attending church and growing in the Lord. This was a spiritual turning point in the Harris family, and the beginning of a strong Christian heritage of worship and service to the Lord! None of us are perfect, but we strive to be more like Christ each day. The verse above holds true, as our family has been blessed through each generation!

But just because you're born into this wonderful family doesn't mean you are automatically a Christian. You have to make that decision for yourself, and ask Jesus to forgive you, and change your heart. Then you will be a part of God's family, which is way better than just being a member of the Harris family.

Week 30

Joy of Grace

by Rebecca Frederick Lambert
Daughter of Lolita Frederick Harris,
the daughter-in-law of Vern Harris

*This will be written for the **generation** to come, that a people yet to be created may praise the Lord. Psalm 102:18 NKJV*

We all experience that season of life in which our focus shifts from those who go before us to those who follow behind. It can be overwhelming, as you place expectations on yourself of living up to some holy standard that will please the Lord and make your kids "want to be like you." (Enter GRACE.) When we recognize we will never be enough and that in our weakness He is strongest, we finally begin to live out what our children need to see. I am convinced that the best thing I can model for my children, nieces and nephews, students and mentees is full RELIANCE on Him. This is certain: I won't always get it right, I will get frustrated, tired, and weak. AND this is also certain:

He is faithful, His grace covers all, His love endures forever, His promises are yes and amen. When I am open about the fact that I am nowhere near perfect, that I need Him, and that He loves me this way, the next generation will know the same is true for them. It sure takes the pressure off when you realize He is the only one who can make us righteous. What joy we find in Abba Father as He raises us up to live out the life He has so intricately designed for us! From that joy comes my favorite part: generations to come will praise the Lord forever!

READ PSALM 102:18-28

Week 31

The Same God

by Robin Acheson Harris
Daughter-in-law of Ralph Harris

*You, O Lord, reign forever; Your throne endures from **generation** to **generation**. Lamentations 5:19 ESV*

Fifty years ago, when I was a child, my grandma would take me to a park near her house to play on the playground. That playground had a merry-go-round that could make you dizzy. There was a real airplane to climb on that had the insides removed. There was a metal slide about 7 feet high. It took great courage to not only climb the ladder but also to slide down the chute from that height. There were a couple of teeter totters that you would have to balance the weight of the kids on each end.

When I took my kids to that same park a generation later, everything had changed. All the playground equipment that I remember was gone. In its place was a new, safer, updated playground.

The almighty God is not like that. His throne endures from generation to generation. He is the same Lord for me that He was for my parents, grandparents, and great-grandparents.

He is the same God who told Noah how to build the ark.

He is the same God who shut the lions' mouths when Daniel was thrown in with them.

He is the same God who revealed Himself to Paul in the blinding light.

He is the same Lord who gave His Son, Jesus, to be the perfect sacrifice to provide salvation for us all.

You, O Lord, reign forever; Your throne endures from generation to generation. Lamentations 5:19

Week 32

Sharing Stories

by Karen Pritchett Sebastian Wirth
Blessed by the Harris Family for over four generations

*"I will put the one who longs for it in a safe place." The words of the Lord are pure words, like silver refined in an earthen furnace, purified seven times. You, Lord, will guard us; You will protect us from this **generation** forever. Psalm 12:5-7 HCSB*

This Psalm is set in a dark place in the life of David. David has been appointed as the next king but was running for his life. Saul had become jealous of David's popularity and was trying to kill him. One day David stopped in Nob to seek refuge and something to eat. Ahimelech, the priest who was in charge, did not know that David was fleeing from Saul and offered him, not only the Bread of Presence but also, the sword of Goliath.

As you face an increasingly wicked world, the Lord provides you with a safe place. The perspective of what is happening in your life (and the lives of those you love) can change as you recognize the refining process and purification in the hard times. There are generational blessings of protection and longevity regardless of the destruction around you. Your provision will come in God's presence as you remember the victories won in the past. Past generations have wonderful stories of the giants they killed, now it is your turn to share yours.

Week 33

Take the Witness Stand, Please!

by Tammy Harris Shaw
Granddaughter of Vern Harris

*Let each **generation** tell its children of your mighty acts; let them proclaim your power. Psalm 145:4 NLT*

A witness is someone who has knowledge about a matter. In the court of law, a witness is someone who, provides testimonial evidence, either oral or written, of what he or she knows or claims to know. There are different kinds of witnesses: an eyewitness, an expert witness, or a character witness.

In Deuteronomy 11, the Bible specifically talks about the Children of Israel being eyewitnesses: "But you have seen the Lord perform all these mighty deeds with your own eyes!" Deuteronomy 11:7 NLT

What have you seen with our own eyes? What mighty things has the Lord done for you? How has He carried you through the valley? We are expert witnesses of our own life! We can affirm and declare the truth of what God has done in us, and for us.

We are not bystanders, onlookers, or observers... we are actual "eyewitnesses" to God's miraculous power in our life. Let's be faithful to share and be witnesses to the generations that surround us, about the mighty acts and power we've seen from the Lord. Imagine how awesome it would be to hear firsthand accounts from Israelite parents of how God opened the Red Sea! We too have those Red Sea moments...

God is always working in our lives. Let us profess and testify of His goodness to our children and grandchildren!

We will not hide these truths from our children; we will tell the next generation about the glorious deeds of the Lord, about his power and his mighty wonders... so the next generation might know them— even the children not yet born— and they in turn will teach their own children. So each generation should set its hope anew on God, not forgetting his glorious miracles and obeying his commands.
Psalm 78:4, 6-7 NLT

Week 34

Blessed to be a Blessing

by Shay Isaac
Granddaughter of Darleene Harris Hemmerling

*"You were willing to offer the Lord your only son, and so he makes you this solemn promise, 'I will bless you and give you such a large family, that someday your descendants will be more numerous than the stars in the sky or the grains of sand along the beach . . . You have obeyed me, and **so you and your descendants will be a blessing to all nations on earth.**'"*
Genesis 22: 16-18 CEV, emphasis added

Can you imagine the Lord's angel calling this out to you from heaven? A promise for all of the nations on earth, fulfilled through your family. Through a very painful sacrifice and subsequent deliverance, Abraham received a sweet foreshadowing of our Lord's saving grace and our adoption into God's family. We know that it is through Jesus, His death and resurrection, that we and all nations on earth are blessed. Today, we can pray for the 3.19 billion people who currently live in parts of the world where they don't even know one Christian, and for Bible translation to be started in the 2,115 remaining languages.

Further Study: Matthew 28:16-20, Revelation 7:19-27, Jesus Gave it All

Reflection:

How is the Lord calling you to bless the nations with Him today?

What sacrifice is required to follow Jesus in sharing the Gospel across cultures?

Do we give Him all? Our time? Our affection? Our sons and daughters? Our comfort?

Application:

Welcome an immigrant neighbour into your home.

Pray for the nations.
(https://prayercast.com, https://joshuaproject.net)

Consider cross cultural living or help in sending another Christian missionary to go.

Prayer:

Lord, thank You for blessing us with a family, and for Your goodness to us. We repent of how we grow apathetic to You, Your love, and Your call to care for the nations of the world. Show us how to join You in blessing the nations, Lord. We love You. Amen.

Week 35

Your Leadership Expires and is Replaced

by Sherri West Coats
Granddaughter of Glenn Harris

*The people served the Lord throughout the lifetime of Joshua and of the elders who outlived him and who had seen all the great things the Lord had done for Israel... After that whole **generation** had been gathered to their ancestors, another **generation** grew up who knew neither the Lord nor what he had done for Israel.*
Judges 2:7,10 NIV

How did this happen?!?! Of all the groups of people in the Bible, Moses, Joshua and the children of Israel saw more of God's mighty hand in the form of miracles, purpose, and provision than any other group. How then, did the following generation not know the Lord or what He had done?!?!

Father Time is undefeated. The death rate is unchanged: one per person. Just as with Joshua and those in our family who have been gathered to their ancestors, we too will one day be gathered to our ancestors. And with it, our leadership will expire and be replaced. Replaced with what? Whatever the next generation chases after and serves. This is exactly what happened to the children of Israel. In 2020 we are in the same dilemma. Think of the many choices the world offers a generation to chase after and serve today. What a sobering thought!

This theme has become a focus, passion, and mantra in my life as I am now a grandparent to that next generation. *Lord, help me be mindful, purposeful, and intentional in telling the next generation so theirs will be a generation that knows You and what You have done! Amen.*

Week 36

A Living Epistle

by Dave Detter
Grandson-in-law of Glenn Harris

***Generation** after **generation** stands in awe of your work; each one tells stories of your mighty acts. Psalm 145:4 MSG*

Grandma Berta (Roberta Harris) was quite a lady! I remember meeting this incredible woman over 35 years ago. Larry and Angela Harris were about to get married, and Lavonna and I came to Ada, Oklahoma, for me to meet the family. It was Thanksgiving, 1984. I had recently asked Lavonna to marry me, and I knew that grandparents can have much influence in the future of a marriage.

We went over to Grandma Berta's cabin in the morning for breakfast and I wanted to make a good impression. I remember her greeting as a loving embrace and this amazing feeling of honor and welcome. She was so down to earth and easy to talk to that it seemed I knew her my whole life. She exuded this innate spiritual strength that had a very settling affect upon me. Her faith in God was obvious, but it was more than that. There was a grace, love, and acceptance that showed me the likeness of Jesus. Her laugh and smile were contagious with just the hint of a mischievous twinkle in her eyes. Just before we left she grabbed my hand and said she wanted to pray for us. Wow! It was obvious that this woman was a spiritual powerhouse—an anchor not swayed by life's ups and downs as she acknowledged a sovereign God.

Roberta Harris not only shared stories of God's mighty acts. She was what the Apostle Paul calls a "Living Epistle" (2 Corinthians 3:2) that inscribed the life of Jesus onto the hearts of everyone who knew her. She stood in awe of God's work! Each of us can also influence the next generation(s) as we stand in awe of His work, tell stories of His mighty acts, and exude God's grace, love, and acceptance that reveals more of the likeness of Christ.

Week 37

by Steve Hartman
Nephew of Marilyn Harris West, the daughter of Glenn Harris

*I will sing of the Lord's great love forever;
with my mouth I will make your faithfulness
known through all **generations**. Psalm 89:1 NIV*

I remember hearing Grandma sing. She sang over all of us; to every baby she held in her arms to bring them comfort (bye, oh baby bye!). I also heard her pray and cry out to God on numerous occasions to help her children or grandchildren. She had a direct line and, thankfully, she shared that number with all of us. We are all grown up now and making the same calls to God, singing the same songs, and crying out for God's help. We are so blessed to have heard these songs, prayers and sweet melodies from grandparents, parents, aunts and uncles.

Like most people, we have had our share of heartaches and challenges; things haven't always gone as planned. But we have known His love and seen

His faithfulness to our family, again and again. When everything in life is shaken, we run to Him and cry out for help, just like we learned from those who loved us and raised us. Our children get to see and learn from our response to life's ups and downs; they hear our song. We are making His faithfulness known to them and their children.

I am forever thankful that I grew up hearing loved ones singing songs of His love. I'm still growing up and I'll keep singing!

Week 38

"I Got This"

by Tim Phelps
Great-nephew to Glenn Harris

***Generation** after **generation** stands in awe of your work; each one tells stories of your mighty works.*
Psalm 145:4 MSG

Have you ever wondered why something is taking so long? Have you ever wondered why the Bible tells us to wait?

We know God has given us a future and a hope but some days it just seems very long and you just want to give up and settle. But I decided to wait on Him for His timing. In the waiting, I lived each day and enjoyed each day for what God had planned for me—just that day. My answer did come on December 2nd with an American Airlines badge in my hand on January 10th.

"Lord, thank You for guiding me through my life and letting me learn from those who have blazed the trail before me so that I grow up in the waiting time. I am now ready for what You have planned for me all along and to show my generation how good You are."

Week 39

Royal Heirs

by Jesse Lambert
Son-in-law of Lolita Frederick Harris,
the daughter-in-law of Vern Harris

We are reborn into a perfect inheritance that can never perish, never be defiled, and never diminish. It is promised and preserved forever in the heavenly realm for you! Through our faith, the mighty power of God constantly guards us until our full salvation is ready to be revealed in the last time. 1 Peter 1:4-5 TPT

Take a moment to focus on the fact that you are promised a perfect inheritance that cannot be altered in any way. You are an heir to the throne, which makes you royalty. "Now if we are children, then we are heirs—heirs of God and co-heirs with Christ," Romans 8:17. "Do not be afraid, little flock, for your Father has been pleased to give you the kingdom." (Luke 12:32) Being part of a royal family comes with its privileges. Even though you are not the King, you get to walk in the authority of the King! I challenge you to take a Royal perspective, stand strong on the Word of God, and through faith walk in His authority knowing that you are an heir and co-heir of His Kingdom.

Week 40

Watchful Anticipation

by Terry Tamashiro Harris
Granddaughter-in-law of Glenn Harris

*I will make sure the fame of your name is honored in every **generation** as all the people praise you, giving you thanks forever and ever!*
Psalm 45:17 TPT

Grandma Berta leaned forward, focusing her full attention on me, and smiled in anticipation. "Tell me, what has the Lord been doing in you lately?"

She had the same question every time we visited. In her mind, there was no question of *whether* the Lord was up to something in someone's life, but rather, *what*. It always made me pause to think... more than a little self-consciously. Roberta Harris was a giant in the faith. She prayed for cars to be healed and they were. (Yes, you read that right—it involved being stranded by the road and Grandpa Glenn trying to fix the car.) She saw a goiter on a lady's neck shrink right before her eyes. She even witnessed the healing of someone who was born with one leg shorter than the other. She watched the shorter leg grow to the same length right in front of her. How would anything in my experience even compare?

These giants of the faith in this family (there were and are many of them) understood that Jesus Christ is the same yesterday, today, and forever. There is no limit to His power and no bounds to His love—across all generations. Eagerly, they looked to Him, watching for His every move, confident that He worked as powerfully in the daily moments as He did in the extraordinary ones. The key, it seems, was that watchful expectation—knowing, trusting that He is always up to something good—and being excited and thankful for the big and the small.

So, what has the Lord been doing in you lately?

Father, I praise You for being the loving God You are who is personally and constantly involved in our lives. Forgive me for taking You for granted and overlooking the every day things You do. May I be ever watchful of You, what You're doing around me, and what You want to do through me. Keep me sensitive to Your Spirit so that I will be ready to move when You move. Increase my faith and embolden me to share You with others and believe You for all things—the big and the little. In Jesus' name, Amen.

Week 41

Wisdom of Old

by Stephen Phelps
Great-nephew of Glenn Harris

*"Remember the days of old,
Consider the years of all **generations**.
Ask your father, and he will inform you,
Your elders, and they will tell you."
Deuteronomy 32:7 NKJV*

Every now and then you can come across something you watch that makes you step back and consider the weight you give to parts of your life. I recently watched a video on YouTube that was concerning Alzheimer's, and it made me think long and hard about how well I valued the wisdom and memories of previous generations. There was a portion of the video where he talked about if you can imagine the hands of a clock. The amount of time we as humans have been able to record memories is equivalent to the distance traveled by the hour hand in one second. The staggering realization of how deep and important memories are to our existence stopped me in my tracks. The wealth of knowledge and stories that can enrich your life is incalculable if you reach out to your elders.

We are told in Job 8:8 to "Please inquire of past generations, and consider the things searched out by their fathers." Just imagine the untold decades worth of knowledge you can gain from just sitting down and asking for mentorship from parents, grandparents, great-grandparents, aunts and uncles, cousins, and so on. There is no way to know how much there is to learn if you don't go and seek out the wisdom of previous generations.

Deuteronomy 32:2 puts it so succinctly: "Let my teaching drop as the rain, My speech distill as the dew, As the droplets on the fresh grass and as the showers on the herb."

The funny thing about wisdom shared is it may not bear fruit right away. It may take time, but cherish what those who came before can pass on to you.

Week 42

Reaching New Heights

by Dave Detter
Grandson-in-law of Glenn Harris

*To Him be the glory in the church and in Christ Jesus to all **generations** forever and ever. Amen. Ephesians 3:21 NASB*

It was January 11, 2017 around 9pm. We were in our home when all of a sudden the earth began to shake. Earthquake!? No. A giant 180 foot Eucalyptus tree exploded as it landed 20 feet from our home. We moved shortly thereafter!

During the rainy season, a Eucalyptus will draw all the water for itself and become top heavy. In a grove with their shallow, independent root system, they are prone to fall and simultaneously weaken the other trees in their grove.

The antithesis of this self-absorbed, lone-wolf, energy-sapping Eucalyptus is the Coastal Redwood tree. Each tree is part of a grove of Redwoods with an interdependent root system that can travel up to 100 feet and literally entwines, fuses, and shares vital nutrients to enable them to grow to staggering heights. As I look at the grove of giant 200 plus foot Redwoods surrounding our new home, I notice the young saplings at their base that are protected, fed and enabled to thrive under the umbrella of the older, more seasoned trees. At the same time, the young saplings are contributing to the strength and vitality of the entire grove. This intergenerational dynamic between the younger and older trees displays the life God meant between the different generations in the body of Christ.

How connected are we to others in the church that hail from other generations? The Builders, Boomers, Gen X, Millennials, and Gen Z all have unique strengths. If you study the core values of each generation, you'll find some very different ways they do "life". The question is, do we truly appreciate these differences enough to engage and learn from each other via vital relationships?

Through the kingdom dynamics of grace, humility, love and transparency, all of us can reach new heights! The result? A display of His "glory in the church and in Christ Jesus throughout all generations!" Ephesians 3:21

Week 43

Shine Jesus

by Brenda Frederick Truett
Daughter of Lolita Frederick Harris,
the daughter-in-law of Vern Harris

*"In the Tent of Meeting, outside the curtain that is in front of the Testimony, Aaron and his sons are to keep the lamps burning before the Lord from evening till morning. This is to be a lasting ordinance among the Israelites for the **generations** to come." Exodus 27:21 NIV*

"You are the light of the world... let your light shine before men, that they may see your good deeds and praise your Father in heaven." Matthew 5:14, 16 NIV

In the Old Testament, the priests were in charge of keeping the lamps burning. The Old Testament sacrificial and Temple systems have been abolished, but, as followers of Jesus, we are part of a royal priesthood. According to Jesus, we are now the lampkeepers, and as royal priests we are responsible for ensuring that the light continues burning from generation to generation.

Our responsibility goes beyond our own blood generations, it is also to the generations of the world. It is part of the Great Commission: go and make disciples of all nations. Jesus is the light of the world. He is the source of our light, the light that has guided and blessed our families for generations. I challenge you to be generous with the light, let Jesus shine wherever you go and pierce the darkness of as many as possible who have not yet had the opportunity to encounter Him.

Week 44

Generationally Influenced

by Steve Harris
Son of Vern Harris

*The book of **generation** of Jesus Christ,
the son of David, the son of Abraham.
Matthew 1:1 KJV*

Reading the Bible, we often skip over genealogies. The record of Jesus' generations are very important because of who He is and the prophetic promises made about His life and purpose. He had to be in the lineage of David to be a king, for instance. Matthew presents Jesus as a king, so His generations must prove that He had the proper pedigree to claim the throne.

Luke presents Jesus as the son of man, His human side. The origins of a man helps us know where he is coming from. Don't skip over Jesus' genealogy too quickly; look closely. Carlisle Marney describes the impact and influence people have on our lives: "All of us are shaped by the people in our cellar and in our balcony."

Luke reminds us of the people in Jesus' cellar and balcony. Here are a few, but you could make a list of all the cellar/balcony people in Jesus' generations, and each would give you a special message about their pilgrimage with God.

Adam: when we are disobedient, God still loves us and cares.

Noah: follow God's guidance, going against the crowd even when they laugh.

Abraham: left the safe and familiar to follow God.

Jacob: got off to a bad start in life, finally letting God give him a new name.

Esther, Joseph, David, there are so many more... You get the picture.

Consider making a list of cellar or balcony people in your generations, and how their qualities have influenced your life.

Week 45

Seeking God

by Sherri West Coats
Granddaughter of Glenn Harris

*They will receive blessing from the Lord and vindication from God their Savior. Such is the **generation** of those who seek him, who seek your face, God of Jacob. Psalm 24:5-6 NIV*

A grandparent who seeks God in front of the generations who follow is a gift! My grandparents, Glenn and Roberta Harris, were a generation who were consistent in seeking God! I have vivid memories of growing up watching my grandparents live out their lives in just this way. It wasn't in large displays, but in the little and steadfast activities of their daily lives that made such a great impression on me.

As a child, I learned the Lord's Prayer by joining in their nightly routine with Evelyn in reciting the prayer when I spent the night with them. I attended church on a Sunday night where my grandpa's singing and clapping in praise seemed louder than most. I knelt at the altar with my grandma and listened to her natural conversations with God. I bowed in prayer for traveling mercies that preceded their every road trip.

As a young married adult, we had conversations about financial stewardship over a game of Rummikub or Yahtzee. I watched them give generously to family, the church and wherever they saw a need. Sometimes, we would arrive at their house unannounced to find them sitting at the kitchen table listening to cassette tapes of their favorite Bible teachers or praise music. Through their lifetime of seeking God, they were indeed blessed! I am blessed and forever grateful for their continued influence in my life.

Father, Help me be a generation who seeks You in my daily life and routines. Help me be faithful to lead the next generation to seek after You. Amen.

Week 46

Quivers and Arrows

by Geri Harris Lovelace
Granddaughter of Vern Harris

Children are a heritage from the Lord, offspring a reward from him. Like arrows in the hands of a warrior are children born in one's youth. Blessed is the man whose quiver is full of them. They will not be put to shame when they contend with their opponents in court. Psalm 127:3-5 NIV

As a young man, Jim Elliott, was preparing to go to South America as a missionary. He penned a letter to his parents upon hearing they were distressed about him making the decision to go. In his letter he reminds them of this passage when he says:

"Remember how the Psalmist described children? He said that they were as an heritage from the Lord, and that every man should be happy who had his quiver full of them. And what is a quiver full of but arrows? And what are arrows for but to shoot? So, with the strong arms of prayer, draw the bowstring back and let the arrows fly—all of them, straight at the Enemy's hosts." (Elisabeth Elliot, Shadow of the Almighty: The Life and Testament of Jim Elliot, [New York: Harper & Brothers, Publishers: 1958] p. 132)

I have an indelible image in my childhood memory of my father (Mark Harris) kneeling at the side of his bed pouring out his heart to God in prayer. I watched both he and my mom, Sharon, over my lifetime be faithful in prayer over their children, their family, and those in the churches they pastored. I don't know the details of each prayer but I know the prayer of a righteous man (or woman) is powerful and effective. (James 5:16)

First can I say, thank you, dear older generations of our family, for your prayer over us, your descendants. We are blessed as a result of your faithfulness. Your "strong arm" of prayer, as Jim Elliot describes, has pulled back the bowstring and shot your "arrows" deep into the enemy territory.

My encouragement for all of us to continue praying for our children and our children's children is that God would lead them and empower them to spread the love of Christ far and wide. We have been so blessed as a family with a godly heritage. Blessed to be a blessing to the rest of the world.

Week 47

Immeasurably More

by Shannon Detter Martinez
Great-granddaughter of Glenn Harris

*Now to him who is able to do immeasurably more than all we ask or imagine, according to his power that is at work within us, to him be glory in the church and in Christ Jesus throughout all **generations**, for ever and ever! Amen. Ephesians 3:20-21 NIV*

Sometimes it can be a little intimidating looking at the rich history of our family. Considering, remembering testimonies and how the Lord has used those that have gone before me. Sometimes it can leave me feeling like I am falling short in my work, marriage and relationships with others, my family, strangers, the Lord. I felt like I couldn't write this piece. Today this verse spoke to me in a new way. I felt encouraged. His power was and is at work in us. It is at work in me. I was reminded that God is a personal god. He wants a relationship with ME. He wants a relationship with YOU. A power that is full of healing and victory and grace and joy. A power that does immeasurably more than I could ever even ask for or even imagine. I pray that if you've been feeling lonely or not enough or falling short that reading this scripture is an encouragement to you.

Lord, thank You for Your grace and power. Thank You for knowing me deeply, personally, perfectly. Remind me of the grace and power You have at work in me. Praise and glory to You every day. Amen.

Week 48

Hope Anew

by Justin Truett
Great-grandson-in-law of Glenn Harris

*We will not hide these truths from our children; we will tell the next **generation** about the glorious deeds of the Lord, about his power and his mighty wonders. For he issued his laws to Jacob; he gave his instructions to Israel. He commanded our ancestors to teach them to their children, so the next **generation** might know them— even the children not yet born— and they in turn will teach their own children. So each **generation** should set its hope anew on God, not forgetting his glorious miracles and obeying his commands. Psalm 78:4-7 NLT*

There are many beautiful things that we can inherit from our family, and many of us have benefited from the labor of those who have come before us. There is one thing, though, that we cannot inherit from preceding generations... Faith. Our faith in God is not something that can be handed from one person to another.

It can be offered, taught, encouraged, and so on, but it cannot be inherited. Unfortunately, there are a lot of people that walk around thinking that they are okay with God because their parents were Christians.

"So each generation should set its hope ANEW on God..." Each generation has a responsibility to decide for themselves whether or not they will follow the Lord. Why? The success in our walk with the Lord is determined by our proximity to Him. That's because He wants a close, personal relationship with us, and that responsibility can only fall on individuals.

We also have the responsibility to teach the next generation about our experiences with God. Our story about our walk with the Lord is our testimony, and our testimony should be what encourages our children to believe for themselves. When we walk closely with the Lord and in His power, it gives overwhelming evidence for the existence of a good and personal God. So find out who God is for yourself, and when you do, walk so closely with Him that the generations that follow you are compelled to do the same.

Week 49

Humble Beginnings

by Wayne Harris
Grandson of Glenn Harris

*How joyful are those that fear the Lord
and delight in obeying His commands.
Their children will be successful everywhere;
an entire **generation** of godly people
will be blessed. Psalm 112:1-2 NLT*

In the mid-1940s, two brothers decided they wanted to make a difference in the world. They didn't have money, they didn't have a title, they didn't have any exceptional skills. All they had was a dump truck and the desire to impact the world for God's Kingdom. They decided to use that truck to earn money so they could give to missions. That one truck multiplied to two trucks, and then three, until there were hundreds. All the while, they gave to the program they created: Missionary Assist Program.

Fast forward 50 years after my grandfather and great uncle started Harris Transportation... Bill Sebastian, a former Missionary Assist, became my pastor and spiritual mentor when I moved to Texas. The seeds that were sown so many years before produced fruit in my life. In Zechariah 4:10, it says not to despise humble beginnings, and Psalm 112:1-2 says, "How joyful are those that fear the Lord and delight in obeying His commands. Their children will be successful everywhere; an entire generation of godly people will be blessed."

What humble beginnings has God prompted you with?

Can you imagine the impact on future generations from your faithfulness. . .or the lack of impact if you don't start?

Today is the day to start.

Week 50

Joyful Obedience

by Tiffany West
Great-granddaughter of Glenn Harris

Praise the LORD!
How joyful are those who fear the LORD
and delight in obeying his commands.
Their children will be successful everywhere;
*an entire **generation** of godly people will be blessed.*
They themselves will be wealthy,
and their good deeds will last forever.
Psalm 112:1-3 NLT

God has been constantly faithful to me, and I fear Him more every day. As a kid, I always thought of the fear of God as "fire and brimstone." I didn't understand that this was a different kind of fear that is actually about awe and accepting that God is so much bigger than we could ever imagine. Certainly, He does have the capability of bringing fire down on us and we would be deserving, but that is not His heart; He sent

Jesus to take on sin so we could be reunited with Him for eternity.

When we reunite with each other at Ada Connection, I am reminded of the magnitude of our reunion with God and how special it is that the obstacle of sin was overcome so we can meet with Him every single day. Rather than making me "scared" of Him as I understood it as a kid, fear of the Lord gives me immense comfort and security knowing that at all times, He is in control. With that knowledge, we can delight in obeying Him, knowing that He will take care of the outcome because nothing and no one is more powerful than Him.

A group of kids, including Melvin Harris, Darleene Harris, and Steve Harris, obeyed God and invited their friend, my Papu Mike Frederick, to church. Because of that simple act, I am writing this today. My Papu devoted his life to serving God and even his great grandchildren serve the Lord as a result. Make the choice to obey God today; you are likely impacting multiple generations!

Week 51

Motivation

by Dylan Morrish
Great-grandson-in-law of Glenn Harris

*So each **generation** should set its hope anew on God, not forgetting his glorious miracles and obeying his commands. Psalm 78:7 NLT*

This verse prompts and motivates me to pursue two things. First, to pursue and receive openly from the generations before me; to ask of the numerous testimonies of the miracles God has done and the life-giving guidance He has given them. To ask those who have gone before me how God met them, led them, and provided a way where there was none. To come against what pride can arise in me when I come up against a new challenge or difficulty and instead seek what wisdom He has given to the numerous people before me. Secondly, this verse prompts me to remember and share the miracles and life-giving guidance He has given to me. To have these ready like presents of praise and direction for the next generation.

To actively seek to pass along what He has given me. This honor God gives each of us shines brightly as I reflect on this verse: that He would consider each of us worthy to be His means to share with the next generation the fullness of life His ways bring.

Week 52

His Throne Endures

by Christina Bonar Osborne
Great-niece to Marilyn Harris West,
the daughter of Glenn Harris

*But you, O Lord, reign forever;
your throne endures to all **generations**.
Lamentations 5:19 ESV*

As I write this, I am very pregnant with our second child, who could make an appearance at any time. And I wonder, what future will this child see? What will the world look like in a year, five years? We have all seen things in our lives turned inside out over the last few months, and uncertainty has taken center stage. With so many questions, the truth of this verse stands out. As we have experienced strange and trying times, we are reminded of God's sovereignty. In a world of so many questions, it is so reassuring to know that the God we serve is in control and reigns forever. Whatever may come for our generation and future generations, we serve a God who is and will forever be on His throne in control. Where questions and uncertainty may follow, we have the peace of knowing the Creator, Savior, and Provider. He has taken care of generations before us, and His throne will endure to all generations.

Ada Connection Week 2021

Family for Eternity

by David Blenkhorn
Son of Genevieve Harris Debord Blenkhorn

And I saw a new Heaven and a new Earth: for the first Heaven and the first Earth have passed away and the sea is no more. Revelation 21:1

When I read this passage of Scripture, I am reminded of how God will reward ALL Believers, who have withstood all the tests of time. . . and have remained faithful. . . to an eternal home with HIM. He will wipe away every tear. . . no more suffering. . . no more disease. . . no more curse of sin to mess things up. . . ALL Believers will finally be ONE family joined with our Lord & Savior for all eternity. Think of it. . . no more remembrances of how we missed the mark. . . or how we decided to be rebellious. . .We get to live in harmony with each other, the angels and our Heavenly Father. Oh, what joy it will truly be! Amen.

Forrest Jesse Harris (Jan. 14, 1888 — April 5, 1965)
Edith Evelyn Murdy Harris (June 17, 1892 — May 25, 1973)
Married May 9, 1912

Edith Evelyn Murdy Harris & Forrest Jesse Harris

Circa 1941. Back Row: Glenn Harris, Cecil Debord, Florence Harris, Ralph Harris, Nellie May Harris Weidenhamer, Vern Harris; Center Row: Joy Harris, Paul Harris; Front Row: Roberta Harris and Melvin, Genevieve Harris Debord, Forrest Harris, Patsy Harris, Edith Harris and Darleene, Thelma Harris and Steve.

Circa 1949. Back row: Glenn Harris, Robert Weidenhamer, Vern Harris, Forrest Harris, Ralph Harris, Cecil Debord; Center row: Joy Harris, Roberta Harris, Nellie May Harris Weidenhamer, Thelma Harris, Edith Harris, Florence and Lois Harris, Genevieve Harris Debord and Margie Debord, Patsy Harris; Front row: Mark Harris, Melvin Harris, Steve Harris, Paul Harris, Harold Harris, Darleene Harris, Marilyn Harris, Gary Debord

Circa 1970 - Back Row: Glenn Harris, Vern Harris, Ralph Harris
Front Row: Darleene Harris Hemmerling, Patricia Harris Kauffman, Edith Murdy Harris, Genevieve Harris Debord Blenkhorn

This page: Home of Forrest and Edith Harris.

Opposite page: Harris siblings circa 1995. Back Row: Glenn, Vern, Ralph; Front Row: Darleene, Nellie May, Genevieve, Patsy

Author Index

A
Aleta Phelps 16
Asher Lambert 20
Ashley Duncan West 34

B
Beverly Bates 66
Brenda Frederick Truett 98
Brittany West 60

C
Charlotte Epperson Harris 30
Christina Bonar Osborne 116

D
Darleene Harris Hemmerling 22
Dave Detter 86, 96
David Blenkhorn 118
Debbie West Jones 18
Dylan Morrish 114
Dylan West 70

E
Ethan Harris 28

G
Geri Harris Lovelace 104
Gideon Lambert 20

J
Jesse Lambert 91
Jodi Pullen Coats 24
Josh Harris 28
Joy Harris Grady 44
Justin Truett 108

K
Karen Pritchett Sebastian Wirth 78
Katelyn Jones Truett 26
Kathy Pinson 48
Kimberly Ann Harris Ricigliano 32

L
Leahna Frederick West 36
Lolita Gurney Frederick Harris 68
Lori Coats Pirtle 42

M
Margie Debord Lundie 50
Mark Harris 54
Matthew Tamashiro-Harris 40
Melvin Harris 58
Michele Hemmerling Isaac 64

P
Patricia Harris Kauffman 38, 62
Paul Kauffman 72

R
Rebecca Frederick Lambert 74
Robin Acheson Harris 76
Robyn Wisler Harris 56

S
Savannah Jones Daniel 46
Shannon Detter Martinez 106
Shay Isaac 82
Sherri West Coats 18, 84, 102
Stephen Phelps 94
Steve Harris 100
Steve Hartman 88

T
Tammy Harris Shaw 80
Terry Tamashiro Harris 92
Tiffany West 112
Tim Phelps 90

V
Vickie Ragsdale 52

W
Wayne Harris 110

www.ingramcontent.com/pod-product-compliance
Lightning Source LLC
Chambersburg PA
CBHW070039230426
43661CB00034B/1437/J